February

Julie Murray

Abdo
MONTHS
Kids

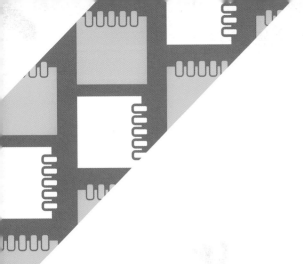

abdopublishing.com

Published by Abdo Kids, a division of ABDO, PO Box 398166, Minneapolis, Minnesota 55439.
Copyright © 2018 by Abdo Consulting Group, Inc. International copyrights reserved in all countries.
No part of this book may be reproduced in any form without written permission from the publisher.

Printed in the United States of America, North Mankato, Minnesota.

052017

092017

THIS BOOK CONTAINS
RECYCLED MATERIALS

Photo Credits: AP Images, iStock, Shutterstock

Production Contributors: Teddy Borth, Jennie Forsberg, Grace Hansen

Design Contributors: Christina Doffing, Candice Keimig, Dorothy Toth

Publisher's Cataloging in Publication Data

Names: Murray, Julie, 1969-, author.

Title: February / by Julie Murray.

Description: Minneapolis, Minnesota : Abdo Kids, 2018 | Series: Months |
    Includes bibliographical references and index.

Identifiers: LCCN 2016962333 | ISBN 9781532100161 (lib. bdg.) |
    ISBN 9781532100857 (ebook) | ISBN 9781532101403 (Read-to-me ebook)

Subjects: LCSH: February (Month)--Juvenile literature. | Calendar--Juvenile literature.

Classification: DDC 398/.33--dc23

LC record available at http://lccn.loc.gov/2016962333

Table of Contents

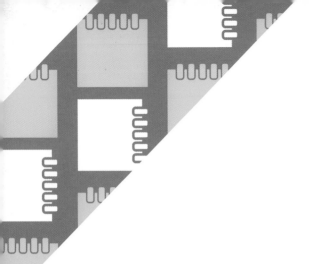

February

There are 12 months in the year.

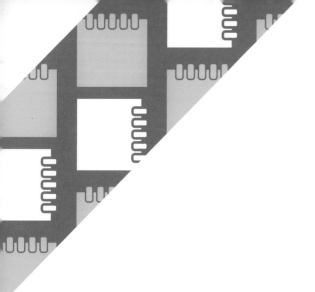

February is the 2nd month. It is short. It only has 28 days.

February

1	2	3	4	5	6	7
8	9	10	11	12	13	14
15	16	17	18	19	20	21
22	23	24	25	26	27	28

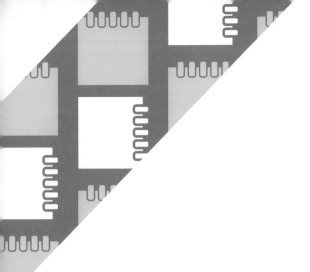

It has 29 days every four years.

It is a leap year!

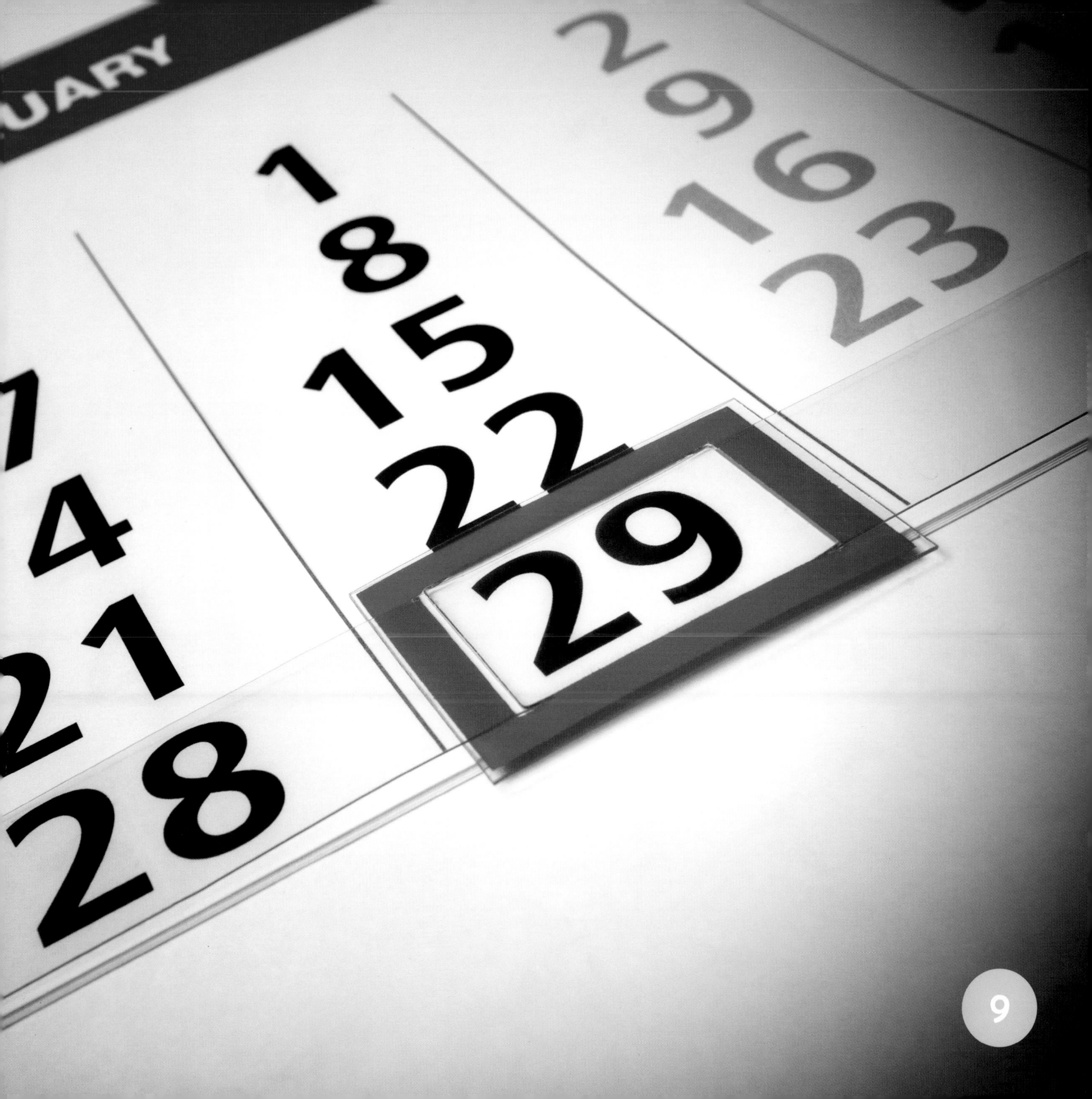
UARY
1
8
15
22
29
7
14
21
28
2
9
16
23

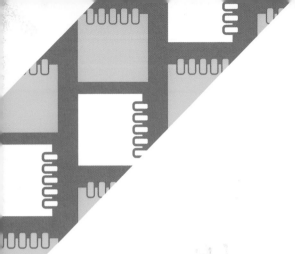

How long will winter last? Find out on Groundhog Day. It is on the 2nd.

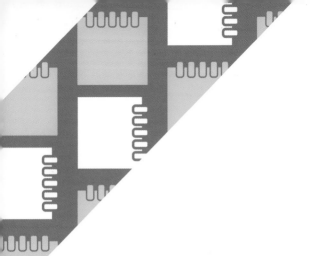

Valentine's Day is fun! It is on the 14th. Finn gives his mom a card.

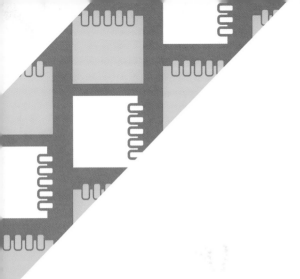

It is **Black History Month**. We learn about great people.

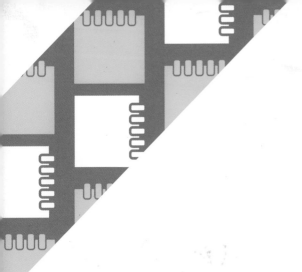

Presidents' Day is the third Monday. We honor our leaders.

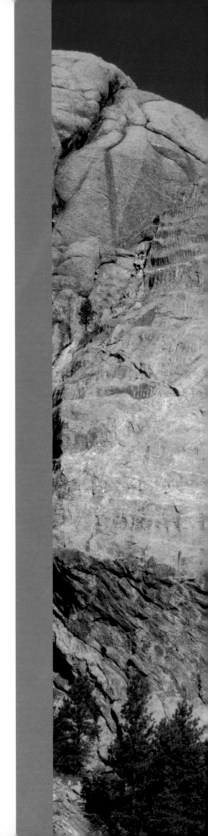

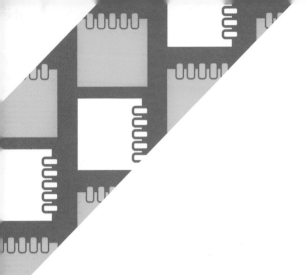

Grace lives in Utah. She skis.

It is fun!

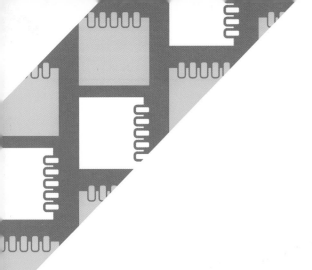

Bob sips hot cocoa.

He loves February!

Fun Days in February

National Pizza Day
February 9

National Inventors' Day
February 11

Susan B. Anthony Day
February 15

National Banana Bread Day
February 23

Glossary

Black History Month
a month that celebrates the achievements of black Americans.

Groundhog Day
a fun day where if a groundhog sees its shadow, people believe winter will last 6 more weeks.

leap year
a year containing 366 days with February 29 as the extra day.

Index

abdokids.com

Use this code to log on to abdokids.com and access crafts, games, videos, and more!

Abdo Kids Code:
MFK0161

24